Visions of Queen

WP
WYMER
PUBLISHING
Bedford, England

First published in Great Britain in 2014
by Wymer Publishing
www.wymerpublishing.co.uk
Wymer Publishing is a trading name of Wymer (UK) Ltd
Tel: 01234 326691

ISBN: 978-1-908724-21-2

Designed and typeset by Andy Francis.
Printed and bound by Ajanta Offset.

A catalogue record for this book is available from the British Library.

Visions of Queen

Bruce Murray (centre) with Victory Rana (left) and Farrokh Bulsara (right) in their first group The Hectics at St Peter's school in Panchgani, a quaint hill-town sixty miles south of Pune. Nobody then imagined Farrokh Bulsara would go on to become a rock star. But Freddie Mercury, as the world came to worship him, with Brian, Roger and John as Queen, established themselves as one of the greatest and most successful bands of all time.

Foreword

It was a huge surprise to be asked to write the foreword to this wonderful book, but then it dawned on me that I had never written anything like this before and I began to panic. I had to dig really deep into the recess of my memory about the young Fred Bulsara as we called him in those days gone by. I remember him as very shy, but very funny in his own way. But of course the one thing that stood out about this shy boy was his piano playing. We used to stand outside the teacher's rest room and listen to the hit parade of those days. Fred would listen to a song once and sit down at the piano and play any song we chose. It was just amazing that he could do this because his music teacher used to despair that he would never learn the proper music pieces she wanted him to. We were fourteen and fifteen at the time and music was our only release from our everyday schoolboy lives.

The year 1960/61: I'm sure it was the same for every kid, all around the world, with any kind of musical bent. All they wanted to be was like their idols Elvis, Cliff, Little Richard, or Fats Domino. I could go on forever naming the pop stars of the late fifties and early sixties. The big difference was that we happened to be five young lads in a boarding school in Pancghani, India. Like so many other wannabe rock stars we just said, "Hey, let's form a band," so we invented The Hectics. With the help of our teachers and parents we managed to buy a bass drum and a snare. I had a guitar, if you could call it that. Little did I know that one day I would own a music store and sell guitars by the bucket load (www.musiccentre.co.uk).

Our bass was a tea chest with a piece of rope, which you plucked on; a great invention because you were always in the right key. The band was made up of Fred Bulsara (piano); (future actor) Derrick Branche, my best friend (mouth organ and vocals) and Victory Rana (drums). Now his is a story I would love to tell. He ended up a major general in the Nepalese Army commanding the UN forces in Cyprus. Completing the band was a guy called Farang Irani (bass box) – who hadn't an inkling about Western music, but he was our mate, so he was in – and me on vocals. The big problem was that none of us could actually play an instrument except for our Fred. Anyway, we managed to conjure up some songs like 'Girl of My Best Friend', 'Yakety Yak', 'Ramona' and some other songs, and believe it or not they actually sounded okay. We played at fêtes in the school and the girls that came from the surrounding schools thought we were pretty cool. They had obviously seen the girls in the movies screaming at their pop idols, so they thought it only right to scream at their local heroes.

Moving on to England 1974, I think that was the year, I went to the Rainbow Theatre, Finsbury Park, to see Queen. What I saw was a superstar in the making and not a young shy lad called Fred Bulsara. Fred had morphed into this thing called Freddie Mercury, but when we hooked up backstage he was still my old schoolmate Fred. This was when I first met up with Brian, Roger and John. We hung out for a while after that. I used to drive him around because I was a minicab driver at the time and actually owned a car. He couldn't drive and he certainly couldn't afford cabs at the time. Even though *Queen* was out and they were pulling in big crowds they didn't have any money coming in. This was at the time they were trying to get away from Trident.

The years flew by and Queen became the biggest band on the planet. I got married, had a child and had moved out of London, so we didn't see much of each other. The last time I saw Freddie and the others was backstage at The Sahara Hotel in Las Vegas. My mother lived there and I was visiting her – it just happened that Queen were in town playing. So I went with my then wife and caught their act and hooked up with them backstage. But by then I think Fred had moved on to being Freddie Mercury for real. He was very friendly and we had a long chat but then he was gone. I never saw him again. When I heard he had Aids, and this was long before the world knew, I was so sad. Mary Austin said to me once, when they were breaking up, "Bruce, you should stick with him. He loves and trusts you." But I didn't and over the years I have always wondered if I would have made a difference to how things turned out. We will never know. But I'm proud of the fact that we knew each other and privileged to have had him as a friend.

With Queen he has given us the best music (probably) the world will ever hear. But then I'm slightly biased. "Sometimes I think back to the old days when we were young."

Bruce Murray

The first time I photographed Queen was towards the start of the winter 1975 UK Tour in Coventry. I can't recall exactly how it all came about now, but the band was promoting the *A Night at the Opera* album, although it was not released until a few days after this concert. That is largely why I was asked to photograph the band so early in the tour as photos were needed to help promote the upcoming dates.

I caught up with them again at Hammersmith Odeon later in the tour and took both monochrome and colour shots at that show. My photo of Freddie on page 26 has become an iconic image, much seen around the world and used on an official Queen T-shirt, while most of the other images have never been seen before.

It was great to have the opportunity to photograph Queen at this stage of their career, before they went on to be a huge phenomenon, as it certainly kick-started my own career and I think some of my best shots were taken on this tour.

Steve Emberton

1975: *A Night at the Opera* UK Tour

November

Friday 14th, Empire Theatre, Liverpool
Saturday 15th, Empire Theatre, Liverpool
Sunday 16th, Belgrade Theatre, Coventry
Monday 17th, Colston Hall, Bristol
Tuesday 18th, Colston Hall, Bristol
Wednesday 19th, Capitol Theatre, Cardiff
Friday 21st, Odeon Theatre, Taunton
Sunday 23rd, Winter Gardens, Bournemouth
Monday 24th, Gaumont Theatre, Southampton
Wednesday 26th, Free Trade Hall, Manchester (2 shows)
Saturday 29th, Hammersmith Odeon, London
Sunday 30th, Hammersmith Odeon, London

December

Monday 1st, Hammersmith Odeon, London
Tuesday 2nd, Hammersmith Odeon, London
Wednesday 3rd, Hammersmith Odeon, London
Sunday 7th, Civic Hall, Wolverhampton
Monday 8th, Guildhall, Preston
Tuesday 9th, Odeon, Birmingham
Wednesday 10th, Odeon, Birmingham
Thursday 11th, City Hall, Newcastle
Saturday 13th, Caird Hall, Dundee
Sunday 14th, Capitol Theatre, Aberdeen
Monday 15th, Apollo Theatre, Glasgow
Tuesday 16th, Apollo Theatre, Glasgow
Wednesday 24th, Hammersmith Odeon, London

The songs performed at Coventry were:

Bohemian Rhapsody
Ogre Battle
Sweet Lady
White Queen
Flick of the Wrist
Bohemian Rhapsody
Killer Queen
The March of the Black Queen
Bohemian Rhapsody (Reprise)
Bring Back That Leroy Brown
Son and Daughter
Guitar Solo
Son and Daughter (Reprise)
The Prophet's Song
Doing All Right
Keep Yourself Alive
Seven Seas of Rhye
Liar
In the Lap of the Gods...Revisited
Now I'm Here
Big Spender
Jailhouse Rock
God Save the Queen

VOX
VOX

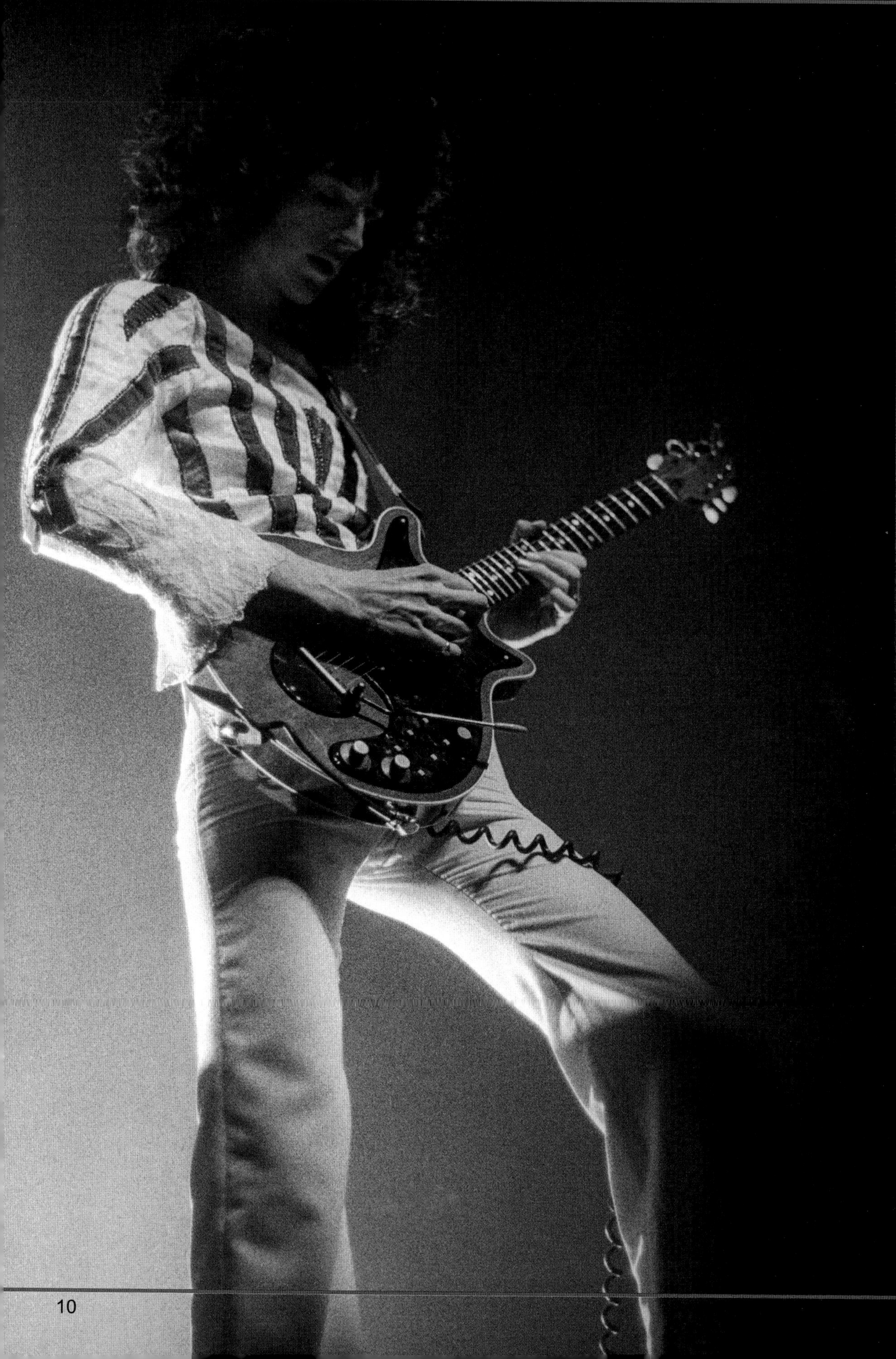

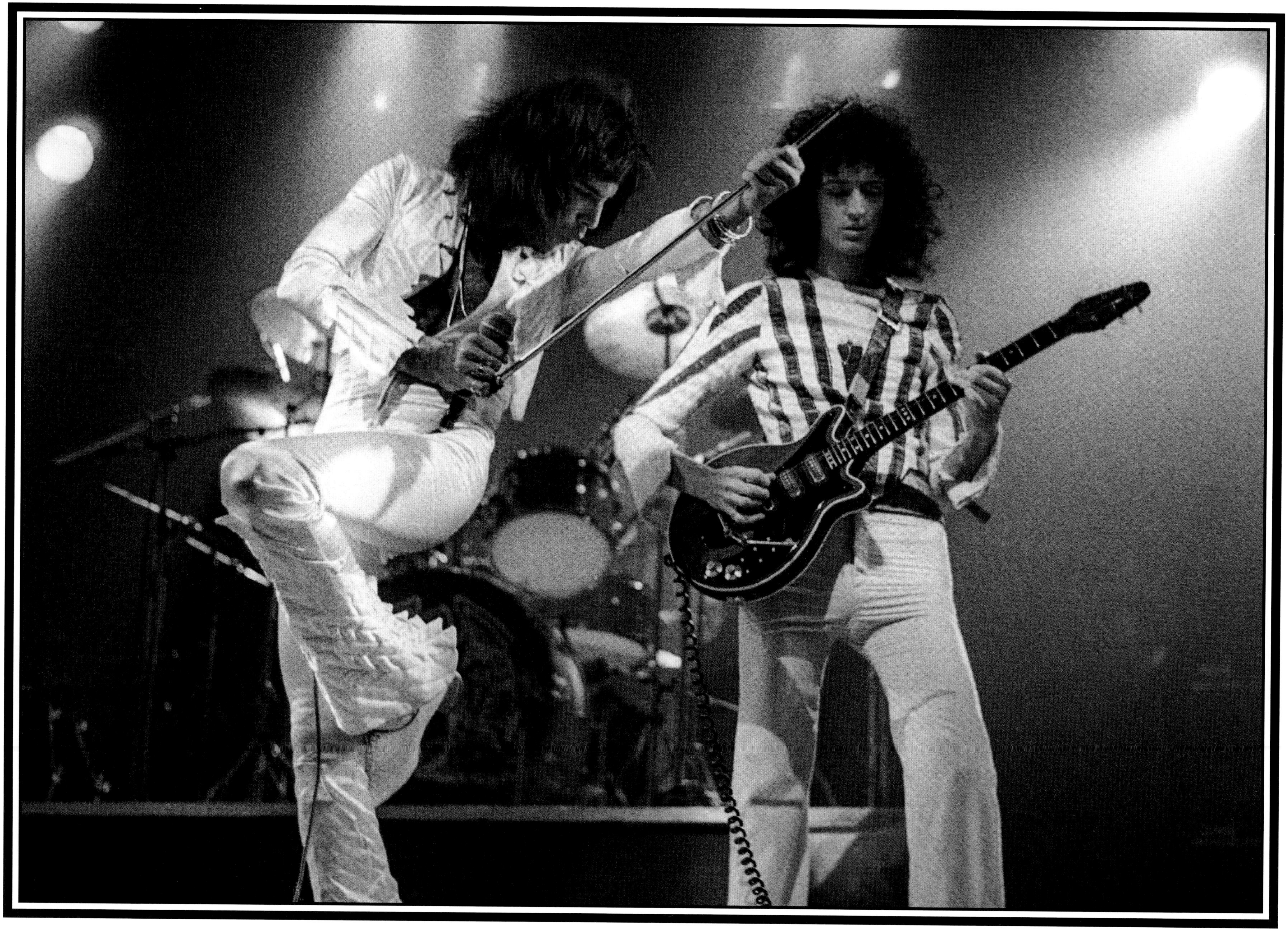

The songs performed at Hammersmith were:

Bohemian Rhapsody
Ogre Battle
Sweet Lady
White Queen
Flick of the Wrist
Bohemian Rhapsody
Killer Queen
The March of the Black Queen
Bohemian Rhapsody (Reprise)
Bring Back That Leroy Brown
Brighton Rock
Guitar Solo
Son and Daughter (Reprise)
The Prophet's Song
Stone Cold Crazy
Doing All Right
Keep Yourself Alive
Modern Times Rock 'n' Roll
Seven Seas of Rhye
Liar
In the Lap of the Gods...Revisited
Now I'm Here
Jailhouse Rock
Be Bop a Lula
Jailhouse Rock (Reprise)
God Save the Queen

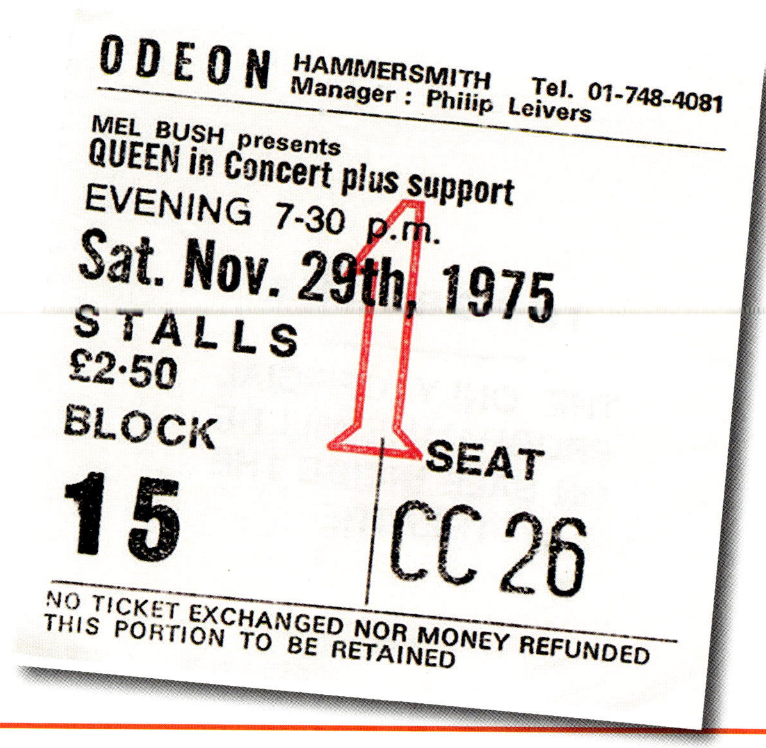
ODEON HAMMERSMITH Tel. 01-748-4081
Manager : Philip Leivers
MEL BUSH presents
QUEEN in Concert plus support
EVENING 7-30 p.m.
Sat. Nov. 29th, 1975
STALLS
£2·50
BLOCK 15
SEAT CC 26
NO TICKET EXCHANGED NOR MONEY REFUNDED
THIS PORTION TO BE RETAINED

Photographing at outdoor shows is never as satisfactory for photographers as indoor venues, and with the stage set up as it was, it meant this was not the easiest of shows for producing great photos. Still, it was an iconic event that I was proud to have had the opportunity to work at. I was by now a staff photographer for Record Mirror, but had also developed a working relationship with Elton John's record company, Rocket Records, and with his and Queen's manager of the time, John Reid. As a consequence of that I also took photos of Rocket Record's signing Kiki Dee at this show.

Steve Emberton

This was the first time I photographed Queen. I went with my then girlfriend, Liz Edwards, who lived in Great Bookham. We arrived by train and navigated using the A–Z of London, the first time that I had seen the publication (I come from Birkenhead and A–Z had not reached there by 1976!). It was a warm, sunny day, and the stage was the same 'Rolling Stones Tongue' that had been used at Knebworth a few weeks earlier.

We arrived whilst Supercharge were playing, starring the crazy Albie Donnelly. Steve Hillage, then Kiki Dee, played as the sun set – she played 'Don't Go Breaking My Heart' with a cardboard cut-out of Elton John. I was quite close to the stage, just to the right of the middle, for the whole concert, so was able to get some reasonable photographs with my Zenit-E with a Vivitar 135mm lens. It was about the seventh concert that I had photographed. I took two films, 80 ASA Kodak negatives.

Alan Perry

1976: Summer UK

September
Wednesday 1st, Playhouse Theatre, Edinburgh
Tuesday 2nd, Playhouse Theatre, Edinburgh
Friday 10th, Cardiff Castle
Saturday 18th, Hyde Park, London

The songs performed at Hyde Park were:

Bohemian Rhapsody
Ogre Battle
Sweet Lady
White Queen
Flick of the Wrist
You're My Best Friend
Bohemian Rhapsody
Killer Queen
The March of the Black Queen
Bohemian Rhapsody (Reprise)
Bring Back That Leroy Brown
Brighton Rock
Guitar Solo
Son and Daughter (Reprise)
'39
You Take My Breath Away
The Prophet's Song
Stone Cold Crazy
Keep Yourself Alive
Liar
In the Lap of the Gods...Revisited

The concert was transmitted live on Capital Radio with DJs Kenny Everett and Nicky Horne.

Having photographed the band a month earlier at Hyde Park, Record Mirror wanted me to attend the *Day at the Races* press launch at the Kempton Park Racecourse at Sunbury-on-Thames, Middlesex.

The photographers all travelled down together in a coach organised by John Reid. It was the only time I photographed the band outside of the concert arena. It was certainly a much more relaxed situation than the gig environment, with more time available to think about composition before taking the shots.

Steve Emberton

1976: *A Day at the Races* press launch

October

Saturday 16th, Kempton Park, Sunbury-on-Thames

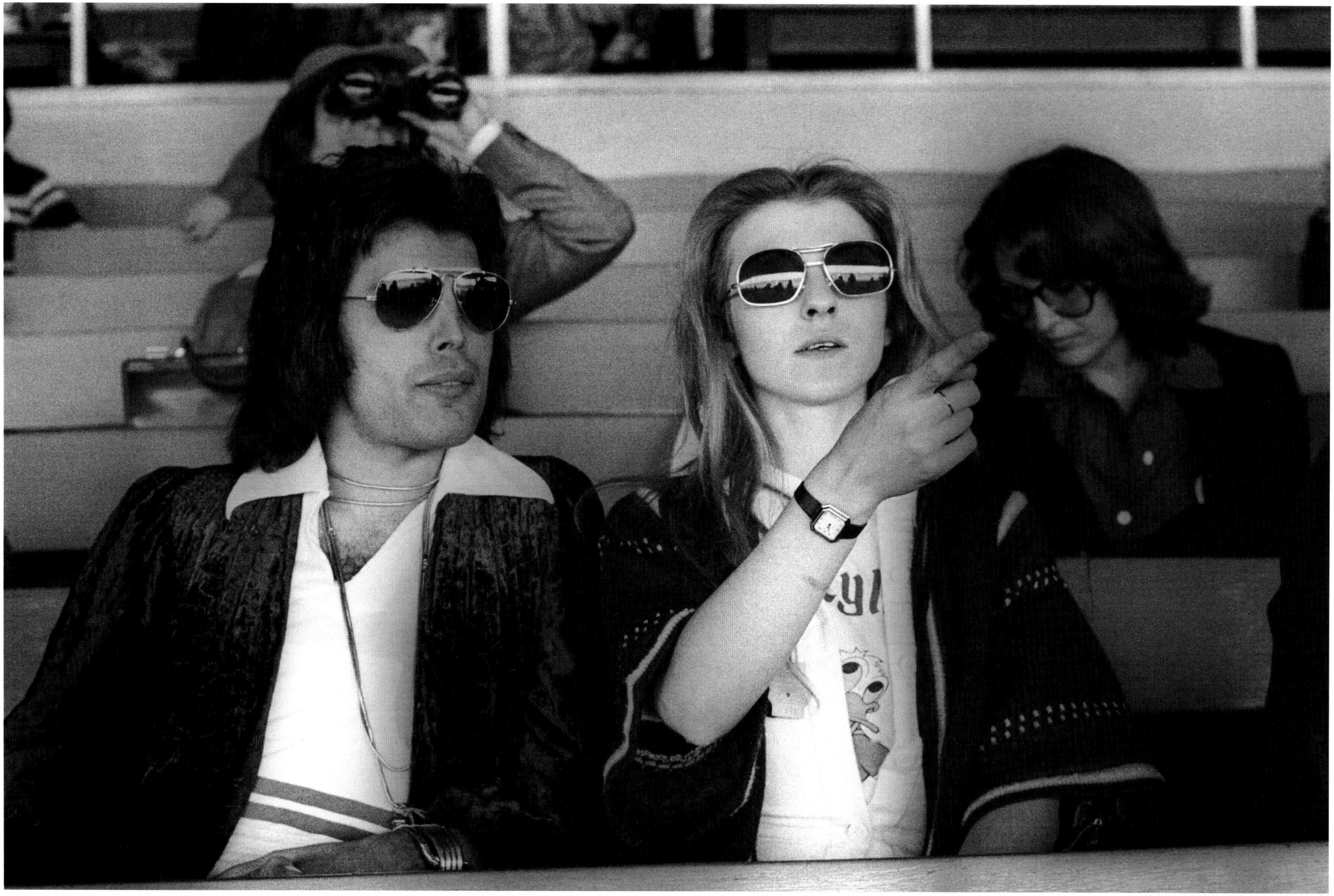

QUEEN
Invite you to:
"A DAY AT THE RACES"
"A Day At The Races" Hurdle Race
Prize money of £3000 donated by
EMI Records and John Reid.
"A Day At The Races" album
available soon on EMI Records.

I captured Brian when he appeared to be deep in thought.

I don't think any of the other photographers took any shots in the dining area, but I'm very pleased of this one of Freddie with Mary Austin, pondering what to have from the menu.

Roger, Brian and John seem less interested in the racing than Mary and Freddie, who is sat next to manager John Reid.

TOTE

John Reid and the band enjoying their day at the races with jockey John Francombe, rider of the winning horse Lanzarote at the 'A Day at the Races Hurdle'. Apparently, unbeknown to each other, the entire band backed Lanzarote to win.

Brian and Freddie behind John Reid who is in conversation with British Olympian hurdle athlete, Alan Pascoe.
Pascoe is wearing his Olympic suit following the Montreal Olympics that summer. He and Brian also have what look like price tags attached to their trousers!

This was the last time I photographed Queen, who by now had moved from the theatres to the larger arenas such as this. Once again I took a mix of monochrome and colour shots, some of which reflect how the band's light show and stage set-up had developed, particularly Roger's drum riser, although the large gong that hung behind him was still only used once at the end of 'Bohemian Rhapsody'.

Steve Emberton

I next photographed Queen on 12 November 1978 at the Empire Pool, Wembley. Roger Taylor came to the front of the stage and played the bass drum on the song ''39'.

I had upgraded my camera to a Canon F1 with a Vivitar 100-300mm zoom by then, and film speed had increased to 100 ASA. Unfortunately I have lost half of the negatives from the 1978 concert.

I travelled to the concert with my friends Jim Boyle and Pete Wakefield and we sold photographs of the Hyde Park concert to the people in the queue. At about midnight we were counting the takings in the Hillman Avenger, which I had borrowed from my father, when a policemen tapped at the window and asked what we were up to!

Alan Perry

1978: *News of the World* UK Tour

May

Saturday 6th, Bingley Hall, Stafford

Sunday 7th, Bingley Hall, Stafford

Thursday 11th, Empire Pool, London

Friday 12th, Empire Pool, London

Saturday 13th, Empire Pool, London

The songs performed at Empire Pool, 11 May were:

We Will Rock You
Brighton Rock
Somebody to Love
Death on Two Legs
Killer Queen
Good Old Fashioned Lover Boy
I'm In Love with My Car
Get Down, Make Love
The Millionaire Waltz
You're My Best Friend
Spread Your Wings
It's Late
Now I'm Here
Love of My Life
'39
My Melancholy Blues
White Man
The Prophet's Song
Guitar Solo
The Prophet's Song (Reprise)
Liar
Bohemian Rhapsody
Keep Yourself Alive
Tie Your Mother Down
We Will Rock You
We Are the Champions
Sheer Heart Attack
Jailhouse Rock
God Save the Queen

The songs performed at Empire Pool, 12 May were:

We Will Rock You
Brighton Rock
Somebody to Love
Death on Two Legs
Killer Queen
Good Old Fashioned Lover Boy
I'm In Love with My Car
Get Down, Make Love
The Millionaire Waltz
You're My Best Friend
Spread Your Wings
It's Late
Now I'm Here
Love of My Life
'39
My Melancholy Blues
White Man
The Prophet's Song
Guitar Solo
The Prophet's Song (Reprise)
Liar
Bohemian Rhapsody
Keep Yourself Alive
Tie Your Mother Down
We Will Rock You
We Are the Champions
Sheer Heart Attack
Jailhouse Rock
God Save the Queen

Queen played at Manchester Apollo on their *Crazy* Tour, playing nineteen gigs in the UK and one in Ireland. One of the central numbers was 'Crazy Little Thing Called Love', which consisted of Freddie Mercury with an Ovation twelve-string guitar to perform this piece. Often the audience thought it was a joke as Freddie was not typically known as being a guitar player. However, he could indeed play, and even if he was very modest about his guitar technique (he often introduced the song by saying, "I can only play three chords."), he played well.

I drove to the Liverpool concert on 6 December 1979 with my friend Sue Tippin and her then boyfriend – he visited his granny at Upton-on-the-Wirral whilst we watched Queen. I had an extended stay by the stage whilst Freddie was playing the piano, so have quite a few photographs in sequence, including one of him pouting, which is my favourite. The film speed had improved to 400 ASA.

Alan Perry

1979: *Crazy* UK Tour

November

Saturday 24th, National Exhibition Centre, Birmingham
Monday 26th, Apollo Theatre, Manchester
Tuesday 27th, Apollo Theatre, Manchester
Friday 30th, Apollo Theatre, Glasgow

December

Saturday 1st, Apollo Theatre, Glasgow
Monday 3rd, City Hall, Newcastle
Tuesday 4th, City Hall, Newcastle
Thursday 6th, Empire Theatre, Liverpool
Friday 7th, Empire Theatre, Liverpool
Sunday 9th, Hippodrome, Bristol, Hippodrome
Monday 10th, Centre, Brighton
Tuesday 11th, Centre, Brighton

(*Crazy* Tour of London)

Thursday 13th, Lyceum Ballroom
Friday 14th, Rainbow Theatre
Monday 17th, Purley Tiffany's
Wednesday 19th, Tottenham Mayfair
Thursday 20th, Lewisham Odeon
Saturday 22nd, Alexandra Palace
Wednesday 26th, Hammersmith Odeon

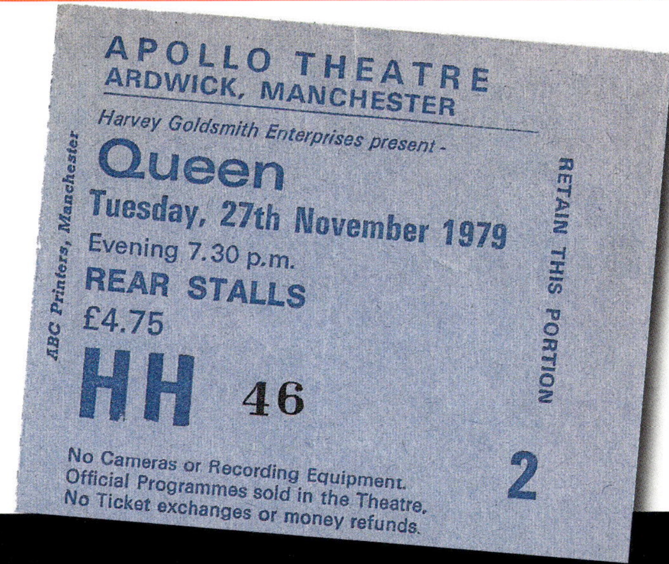
APOLLO THEATRE
ARDWICK, MANCHESTER
Harvey Goldsmith Enterprises present -
Queen
Tuesday, 27th November 1979
Evening 7.30 p.m.
REAR STALLS
£4.75
HH 46
2
No Cameras or Recording Equipment.
Official Programmes sold in the Theatre.
No Ticket exchanges or money refunds.
RETAIN THIS PORTION
ABC Printers, Manchester

VOX

The songs performed at Manchester were:

We Will Rock You
Let Me Entertain You
Somebody to Love
Mustapha
Death on Two Legs
Killer Queen
I'm In Love with My Car
Get Down, Make Love
You're My Best Friend
Save Me
Now I'm Here
Don't Stop Me Now
Spread Your Wings
Love of My Life
'39
Keep Yourself Alive
Guitar Solo
Liar
Crazy Little Thing Called Love
Bohemian Rhapsody
Sheer Heart Attack
We Will Rock You
We Are the Champions
God Save the Queen

BIKE

The songs performed at Liverpool were:

We Will Rock You
Let Me Entertain You
Somebody to Love
Mustapha
Death on Two Legs
Killer Queen
I'm In Love with My Car
Get Down, Make Love
You're My Best Friend
Save Me
Now I'm Here
Don't Stop Me Now
Spread Your Wings
Love of My Life
'39
Fat Bottomed Girls
Keep Yourself Alive
Guitar Solo
Brighton Rock (Reprise)
Crazy Little Thing Called Love
Bohemian Rhapsody
Tie Your Mother Down
Sheer Heart Attack
We Will Rock You
We Are the Champions
God Save the Queen

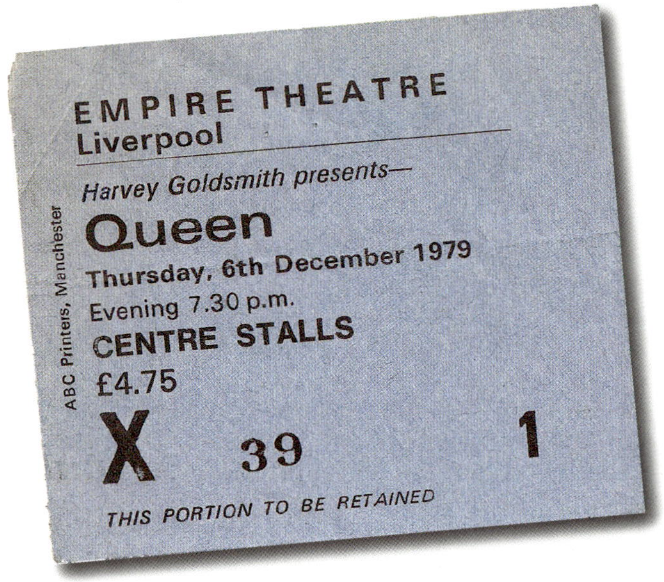

STEVE EMBERTON

Born in Idaho, Steve Emberton joined the US Air Force at the age of seventeen and a few months later he found himself stationed in England. The year was 1964. "England in the sixties was a great place to be," Steve recalls, "with so much happening in the music scene. I just couldn't get enough of it."

Having completed his tour of duty, Steve went back to the US for a few years, but he always had a strong desire to return to England. He did in the early seventies and that was when he decided to make a career of photography. "From an early age I have loved taking pictures of just about anything but my true passion is photographing people. I had the desire but no formal training, so I knew it wasn't going to be easy." He read every book and magazine to do with photography that he could lay his hands on. He studied and practised every chance he got to develop the knowledge and skills he would require. Steve also worked avidly in his home darkroom teaching himself the art of printing.

About a year later he got his first break. A friend suggested he photograph a band that was going to be playing in a local pub. A PR company saw the images and then arranged a photo pass to Don McLean's Hyde Park Concert. By chance Don's manager asked Steve to take some shots of Don and the audience. "One of my images was used full-page in a music paper – *Melody Maker* – and I was on the road to becoming a music photographer."

Steve later became the staff photographer for another music paper, namely *Record Mirror*. He also worked for the *NME*, *Sounds* and other music magazines, newspapers, record labels and PR companies. Over a forty-year career, Steve has photographed pop stars, TV personalities, politicians, actors and models. His work has appeared on album sleeves, in magazines, books, newspapers and on television.

Rolling Stone selected a shot of his of Sid Vicious of The Sex Pistols and his girlfriend Nancy Spungen for its *50th Anniversary of Rock, Fifty Greatest Portraits* Issue (September 2004).

Recently Steve began digitising his seventies music image archive, most of which had never been seen before. Some of these images are now available for use in publications and some are for sale as limited edition prints via his website: www.steveemberton.com.

ALAN PERRY

I started concert photography as a hobby. I have taken thousands of photographs at concerts from 1975 onwards. The first time that I took a camera to a concert was for Genesis at Liverpool, 18 April 1975, but I have no photos of that night. The first thing that I did wrong was to wind the film on so vigorously that the sprockets ripped the film and rendered the camera useless!

I met the group outside the stage door before the concert – they all autographed my album covers. First I spotted Phil walking up Lord Nelson Street towards the stage door. I went up to him and asked him to sign an album cover, which he did. My brother then took a photograph of Phil and me. Everyone else seemed dumbstruck, so I asked him to sign the rest of my album covers, which he did. Tony Banks was in more of a hurry – he asked me where the stage door was and I was the only one to get his autograph. Jill Gabriel arrived with their daughter Anna (who was then a babe in arms). Steve and Mike drove up in a Range Rover. At 7.00 p.m. the roadies were pacing up and down Lord Nelson Street, agitated because Peter had not yet arrived and it was time for the soundcheck. When he did turn up he appeared to be drunk. He signed my album cover and was then engaged in conversation with a fan who explained that he had a recurring dream in which he was Peter Gabriel. Of course Peter found this fascinating, and spent several minutes in conversation, causing the roadies to come close to exploding!

I first saw Queen at Oxford New Theatre on 20 November 1973 when they supported Mott The Hoople. There were about fifty Queen fans congregating at the front of the stalls whilst most people were still in the bar. I remember thinking, "Wow, what is this group!" I was converted into being a fan and subsequently bought all of their albums. The last time I saw them was in 1986 at Knebworth; their last live concert with Freddie Mercury, so I just about spanned their whole live career.
(www.concertphotos.uk.com)

CREDITS

Thanks to Helena Coryndon, Angel Liao & Thomas To at C & C Offset, Pramendra Mehrotra at Ajanta Offset.
Thanks also to Lynn Baker, Greg Brooks, Pete Burridge, Dec Hickey, Bruce Murray, Jacky Smith, Phil Syphe at Grammar Eyes, Greg Taylor, Drew Thompson at Thompson Music Pty, and of course Steve Emberton and Alan Perry for taking the photos in the first place.

Book design and layout by Andy Francis.
Co-ordination by Jerry Bloom at Wymer Publishing.

Photo credits:
St Peter's School, Panchgani, circa 1961, p. 4, courtesy Bruce Murray
Belgrade Theatre, Coventry, 16 November 1975, pp. 8-23 © Steve Emberton
Hammersmith Odeon, London, 29 November 1975, back cover, top & bottom, p. 3, pp. 24-41 © Steve Emberton
Hyde Park, London, 18 September 1976, pp. 44, 46, 48, 49 (monochrome) © Steve Emberton, pp. 45, 47-51 (colour) © Alan Perry
Kempton Park, Day at the Races press launch, 16 October 1976, pp. 54-67 © Steve Emberton
Empire Pool, Wembley, London, 11 May 1978, back cover centre, pp. 70-81, © Steve Emberton
Empire Pool, Wembley, London, 12 May 1978, front cover, pp. 82-87 © Alan Perry
Apollo, Manchester 27 November 1979, pp. 90-103 © Alan Perry
Empire Theatre, Liverpool 6 December 1979, pp. 104-117 © Alan Perry